High-Interest READING

by
Cindy Karwowski

Cover Design by
Matthew Van Zomeren

Inside Illustrations by
Don O'Connor

Publisher
Instructional Fair • TS Denison
Grand Rapids, Michigan 49544

Permission to Reproduce

About the Author

Cindy Karwowski earned her B.A. degree from Carthage College in Kenosha, Wisconsin and her M.A. degree from Michigan State University. A primary teacher with over twenty-five years of experience, she has written several books for Instructional Fair. Cindy has served on numerous curriculum committees, was presented with an Excellence in Teaching Award, and was twice a finalist for Michigan Teacher of the Year.

Credits

Author: Cindy Karwowski
Cover Design: Matthew Van Zomeren
Inside Illustrations: Don O'Connor
Project Director/Editor: Sharon Kirkwood
Editors: Lisa Hancock, Eunice Kuiper
Typesetting/Layout: Pat Geasler

Standard Book Number: 1-56822-611-X
High-Interest Reading
Copyright © 1998 by Instructional Fair • TS Denison
2400 Turner NW
Grand Rapids, Michigan 49544

Table of Contents

Answer Key (in middle of book)

The Ups and Downs of "Yo-yo-ing"

Today yo-yos have become quite popular. Children and adults of all ages may practice for hours in order to perform assorted tricks ranging from "Walk the Dog" to "Eiffel Tower" to "Split the Atom."

Using a yo-yo is not a modern fad. Its history dates back as far as 1000 B.C. The Chinese originated yo-yo-like toys made of two disks carved from ivory with a silk cord wound around a center peg.

The popularity of these toys later spread to Europe. The English called this new plaything a "quiz," and the French referred to it as a "bandalore." These European versions were very special. Many were decorated with jewels and painted in geometric patterns.

In the sixteenth century Philippine hunters created a weapon that they named the "yo-yo," but it was not a toy. It consisted of large wooden disks and strong twine. The hunters used it to snare animals by the legs. When Donald Duncan, an American, saw this Philippine yo-yo in the 1920s, he made it smaller and developed the American toy that today we call the "yo-yo."

1. Read each statement. Write **F** if the statement is a **fact**—something that can be proved. Write **O** if the statement is an **opinion**—what someone believes.

_____ The most difficult yo-yo trick is "Split the Atom."

_____ Yo-yos created in Europe were very beautiful.

_____ Philippine hunters developed a weapon they called a yo-yo.

_____ Early Chinese yo-yos were made of ivory and silk cord.

_____ Everyone enjoys playing with a yo-yo.

_____ Donald Duncan's yo-yo was smaller than the Philippine version.

_____ A person needs years of practice in order to perform difficult tricks using a yo-yo.

2. Fill in the circle that best describes the author's purpose in writing this article.

    ◯ entertain   ◯ inform   ◯ persuade

3. Check the box with the yo-yo that you would be most interested in trying. Then explain the reason why.

    ☐ the Chinese yo-yo   ☐ the Philippine yo-yo

    ☐ the European yo-yo   ☐ a modern yo-yo

Why? _____

_____

_____

Air, Land, and Sea

Look up! Look down! What do you see? If you're a bit daring, your answer may be different from most people's responses.

For example, when people visit the circus, they are amazed at the flying trapeze artists performing high above their heads. These athletes swing, twist, and leap toward the top of the tent or arena as the audience watches intently from the safety of their seats. As astonishing as these flyers may seem, there are some who perform acts even more outlandish!

In 1995, Mike Howard of Great Britain decided to create the highest trapeze act in history. He dazzled his audience at a height of 20,300 feet while suspended from a hot-air balloon! He truly could say that he had a "bird's-eye view" of his audience.

Perhaps you always feel safe as long as you can touch the ground. Maybe you would change your mind if you tried to walk on "Steady Eddy" Wolf's stilts. In 1988, he stood over 40 feet above the ground and walked 25 steps without touching the safety handrail wires!

Maybe you'd feel safest up high knowing that if you fell, you would land in water. That must be how Col. Harry A. Froboess from Switzerland felt. He jumped 394 feet into Lake Constance from an airship! Hmmmm… Perhaps standing on a high diving board is not so scary after all!

1. Circle the main idea of the story.

   - walking on stilts

   - hot-air balloons

   - performing tricks high above the ground

2. Draw a line from each person to his amazing feat.

   Col. Harry A. Froboess   • walked on very tall stilts

   "Steady Eddy" Wolf   • performed a trapeze act while hanging from a hot-air balloon

   Mike Howard   • jumped into water from an airship

3. Answer the riddle by following the directions.

   Why did the diver choose to leap 100 feet down into a glass of soda pop?

   a. Cross out all words in the Word Bank that mean "amazing."

   b. Cross out all words that rhyme with "stilt."

   c. Write the remaining words from bottom to top.

Word Bank
astonishing
built
landings
easy
stunning
quilt
make
drinks
guilt
soft

   _____ _____ _____

   _____ _____

The Wild Visitor

We love to camp in the outdoor air
In open space with room to spare—
Just me and Fuzz, my teddy bear.

We set our tent in no time flat,
Spread out our gear, and there we sat
With lots and lots of time to chat.

We fixed great grub and filled our "tums."
We ate it all—left only crumbs,
Then topped it off with bubble gum.

We closed our eyes and counted sheep,
And just began to fall asleep.
We then felt something start to creep.

It entered through our small tent door.
It stayed down low, close to the floor.
Sweat down our brows began to pour!

We felt its hot breath on our toes.
Its prickly hair brushed past my nose
'Til it lay down upon some clothes.

Now was our chance to get away—
No need to be a wild one's prey—
We ran to the house without delay!

Safe in our home—ol' Fuzz and I
Had racing hearts, we won't deny.
Good thing we're much too brave to cry!

Climbing in bed we snuggled in,
Our heads still in a tailspin.
We heard a noise and had to grin… "Arf! Arf!"

1. Number the events in the correct order.

   _____ A strange visitor entered our tent.

   _____ My friend and I talked and talked.

   _____ Fuzz and I put up the tent.

   _____ My teddy bear and I fell asleep.

   _____ We fixed a delicious dinner.

2. On the line, write the letter of the meaning that matches each word or phrase.

   ___ "no time flat"   a. fall asleep
   ___ "grub"   b. food
   ___ "count sheep"   c. extra space
   ___ "prey"   d. quickly
   ___ "room to spare"   e. hunted animal(s)

3. Circle who you think we thought our visitor(s) might be.

   a. giant lions   c. angry gorillas   e. hungry cougars
   b. big bear   d. wild wolves

Find the animal words above in the puzzle and color those boxes **red**. Color the remaining boxes **black** to discover the name of the visitor. Write its name on this line. _____

S	O	S	B	R	I	G	B	O	E	L	A	M	N	A	R	O	P	D
L	H	U	N	S	G	R	Y	T	C	U	O	R	U	G	A	N	R	S
V	E	G	I	P	A	N	T	X	L	W	I	E	S	O	N	R	D	S
B	A	N	G	I	R	Y	G	D	O	L	R	Y	I	L	L	Q	A	S
M	W	I	L	S	I	R	D	P	L	R	W	X	O	L	V	W	E	S

Patient Pachyderms

BIG! That word definitely describes an elephant. The largest elephant on record measured 13' 8" tall and weighed 13½ tons (27,000 lbs.)! That makes the elephant the largest land animal. Despite its huge size and weight, however, an elephant walks on its tiptoes. It can even sneak past nearby hunters without being detected!

An elephant's trunk is a combination of its nose and upper lip. It consists of over 100,000 different muscles! This allows for great flexibility and control. Amazingly, a trunk can hold over two gallons of water.

When you examine an elephant's skin, its thickness is obvious. However, its skin is also very sensitive because it contains many nerve endings. Generally, most elephants have gray bodies, but some appear to be brown or even red. This is caused by an elephant's tendency to roll in mud. The mud protects the elephant's skin from sunburn, drying out, and insect bites.

Two species of elephants still exist—African elephants and Asian elephants. African elephants have larger ears and are heavier and taller than Asian elephants. Both the male and female African elephants have tusks, while normally, only the Asian male elephants have them. Circuses usually employ Asian elephants because they are smaller and easier to tame.

Circle each correct answer.

1. An elephant is able to use its trunk in many different ways because its trunk . . .

> is very long.
> is a combination of its nose and upper lip.
> contains over 100,000 muscles.

2. The result of an elephant walking on its tiptoes means that the elephant can . . .

> almost reach the height of a giraffe.
> walk very quietly.
> climb over large rocks easily.

3. Because an elephant rolls in muddy water it . . .

> can appear to be a different color.
> needs to bathe often.
> is shunned by other animals.

Write each phrase in the correct category.

Phrase Bank

usually only males have tusks   have larger ears

are used more often in circuses   are heavier and taller

African Elephants	**Asian Elephants**
1. _____	1. _____
2. _____	2. _____

Seeing Spots

One morning when Susie awoke she had an idea. "If I use a red marker to draw spots all over me, I won't have to go to school today." So she proceeded to pepper herself with tiny crimson dots. Then she pretended to be asleep.

When her mother came and tried to awaken her, Susie rolled over, and her mother's eyes widened. "Susie, you have the chicken pox! You won't be able to go anywhere for several days." Then she covered Susie with the blanket, kissed her on her spotted nose, and left the room.

"This is great!" thought Susie. "Now I'll be able to play all day." As she left her bed, she heard footsteps in the hall outside her door. Quickly she dove back beneath the covers. Her mother and Mrs. No-Nonsense, the next-door neighbor, entered.

"Susie," whispered her mother softly, "Dad, Jimmy, and I have to leave to meet our relatives at the circus. Because we organized the gathering, we don't feel it would be polite to cancel. Just stay in bed. Mrs. No-Nonsense will be here if you need anything. She'll sit in that chair so she'll always be nearby."

Susie's mouth dropped to her chin. She had forgotten that it was Saturday. Now she wouldn't be able to go to the circus. As she lay pouting, Susie noticed Mrs. No-Nonsense bend down and put something in her pocket. Susie suddenly realized that it was the red marker! Mrs. No-Nonsense just smiled slyly, sat down in the nearby rocking chair, and began to read a book. This was just the beginning of a very long day!

1. Use six different colors. Color each pair of spots the same color if the word and phrase mean the same.

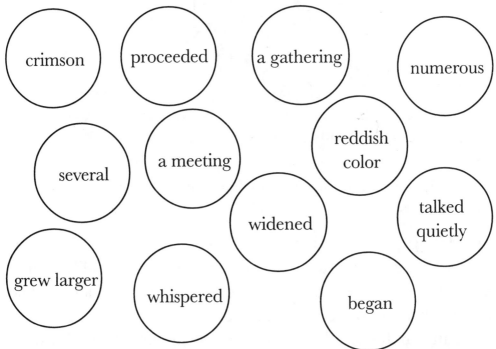

crimson

proceeded

a gathering

numerous

several

a meeting

reddish color

talked quietly

grew larger

widened

whispered

began

2. Underline the statements that are true about this story.

Susie's trick backfired.

Susie didn't have to go to school only because her mother thought she had the chicken pox.

Susie fooled her neighbor.

Susie wasn't happy with the results of her trick.

3. Predict what Susie will do for the rest of the day.

_____

_____

_____

Hairy Situations

"You need a haircut!" say many mothers and fathers to their children. However, some people have found both fame and fortune by not taking their parents' advice. They have even set world records.

If Mata Jagdamba of India ever said, "Sorry, but I can't go out tonight because I have to wash my hair," she was probably telling the truth. In 1994 her hair measured almost 14 feet in length! Did she wear her hair on top of her head, did she carry it, or did she let it hang on the floor behind her? If she just let it hang down, she may have taken many "trips" without going very far.

Most people consider Santa Claus to have quite a beard. Hans N. Langseth of Norway might consider Santa's beard a day's growth, because he grew a beard that measured 17½ feet! It was so unique that it was given to the Smithsonian Institution. It's probably safe to assume that he wasn't often told: "That was a close shave."

Kalyan Ramji Sain of India has long hair, too, but it is not on his head or chin. He proudly wears a mustache that reaches over 11 feet from tip to tip. This makes a person wonder whether he enters a room sideways or if he goes only through very, very wide doorways.

1. Write **F** on the blank if the statement is a fact. Write **O** if the statement is an opinion.

_____ Long hair is very becoming.

_____ In the article, the longest beard measured longer than the widest mustache.

_____ People are very proud of their hair.

_____ A long mustache is silly.

_____ Human hair is much thinner than a pencil.

_____ Short hair is easier to take care of.

_____ People with long hair live longer.

_____ Men with long hair are more handsome.

Circle the correct answer.

2. What do all of the people in the story have in common?

      very long hair

      setting world records for hair growth

      lots of ways to style hair

3. Draw a line to match each person with the gift best suited for him or her.

Hans N. Langseth   mustache wax

Mata Jagdamba   a bib

Kalyan Ramji Sain   barrettes

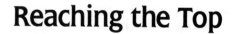

Reaching the Top

There's no problem with my physique—
I could climb to any peak!
I take it just one step each time;
I elevate. And as I climb,
I know my strength and feel my power
As though I'm climbing a tall tower.
Here I go, and as I rise,
I creep up closer to the skies.
Right foot first, and left foot then—
I have the force of fifty men!
My muscles pull, begin to ache.
"Nonsense!" I think, "a piece of cake!"
It's hard to breathe; the air grows thin.
I feel my head begin to spin.
I use my arms to pull me high.
If only they could help me fly,
I will make it to the top,
And when I get there, I will plop
And make a very loud kerplunk!
"Next time I get the bottom bunk!"
I yelled
to
my big
brother
far
below!

1. Circle the main idea of this poem.

   climbing a tall tower

   climbing a mountain

   climbing up to the top bunk

2. Draw a line from each word to its meaning.

   physique   go upward

   peak   very easy

   elevate   strength

   "a piece of cake"   body structure

   force   top of hill or mountain

3. Climb the ladder by reading each clue. Then unscramble and write the word from the poem on each step.

   Clues

   (eowrt)   a tall building

   (tbherae)   to move air in and out of the mouth

   (lcemuss)   body tissue that moves bones

   (rlompbe)   something that needs to be solved

   (soneenns)   a silly thought

Beware!

A newborn *cub* weighs only 8 to 16 ounces and is *blind* and *bald*. Being hairless and unable to see makes a baby bear very *defenseless*. Eventually it grows to become the largest *carnivore* on land. In fact, a polar bear may weigh over 1,750 lbs. And a bear has the largest *molars* of all meat-eating mammals.

All bears, except the polar bear, live on land. Polar bears live part of the time in water. Bears that live in the northern hemispheres may *hibernate* during part of the winter because their food source is unavailable. They *retire* to a *den* or cave to sleep. During this time they live off fat their bodies have stored up.

Different types of bears like to eat different foods. Polar bears *dine* on seals. Brown bears enjoy berries, fish, roots, and dead meat. Pandas feed almost exclusively on bamboo. However, many people do not consider pandas to be bears. Because bears have poor eyesight, they must depend on their keen sense of smell to locate their food.

Although bears are often portrayed in books, movies, and cartoons as cuddly and loving, they can be dangerous creatures. Visitors to parks should not entice bears with food or pet young cubs. This animal can be deadly if it feels threatened.

1. Define each italicized word from the story by writing the letter of its meaning on the blank.

____ cub   a. grinding teeth

____ den   b. spend the winter in dormant state

____ carnivore   c. hairless

____ dine   d. baby bear

____ hibernate   e. unable to see

____ bald   f. eat

____ blind   g. unprotected

____ molars   h. go to sleep

____ retire   i. meat-eater

____ defenseless   j. cave

2. List one food each type of bear enjoys.

   Brown Bear   Panda   Polar Bear

_____   _____   _____

3. List three changes that occur as a bear grows older.

a. _____

b. _____

c. _____

Just My Luck

One day as I was strolling down a path near my house, I looked down at the ground and noticed a small, polished rock glistening in the sun. I picked it up and decided to entertain myself by seeing how far I could throw it. As I sent that rock sailing, I watched it as it landed in the middle of a big patch of green clover. I then went searching for the rock. I ran my fingers through the clover, but I just couldn't find it. I became very disheartened and sighed loudly. I decided to look one last time. My hands pushed away a clump of four-leaf clovers, and that's when I discovered a furry rabbit's foot.

"Well, this has to be my lucky day," I thought aloud. "A rabbit's foot sitting in the middle of four-leaf clovers!" Immediately I began to wonder if it had magic powers. "Hmmm—maybe if I rub it like a magic lamp, something wonderful might occur!" So I placed the foot in my left hand and stroked the soft fur with my right. Nothing happened. I rubbed harder and harder.

All of a sudden my whole body tingled. My limbs began to shake. What was happening? I closed my eyes tightly. When I opened them, I looked down and stared at my feet. They had grown very large and were covered with long, white, silky fur. I touched my cheeks and felt some long, prickly whiskers. When I grabbed my head, I realized what had occurred. I had become a big, white rabbit! Now I could have become quite upset with this situation, but I decided there was nothing I could do to correct it. So I guess I'll just try my best to be *hoppy* and begin looking for lots of carrots.

Circle the correct answer(s) to each question.

1. What lesson did the speaker in the story learn?

   Make the best you can of a situation.

   Do not throw stones or you may hit something.

   Rabbits are magical creatures.

2. What clues indicate how the speaker was changing?

   He found a rabbit's foot.

   His feet grew very large and were covered with fur.

   Whiskers sprouted from his face.

   He was standing in a field of clover.

3. How do you know that the speaker was not too upset?

   He went to sleep.

   He decided to accept the situation.

   His whole body tingled.

Cross out the word in each row that doesn't mean the same as the others.

a.	entertain	amuse	work
b.	happy	weary	disheartened
c.	discovered	lost	found
d.	stroked	rubbed	carried
e.	enormous	situation	circumstance

Yodeling, Yapping, and Rapping

How far can your voice travel? Try yelling to a friend across a room. Then shout to a friend across a large parking lot. Finally, call to your friend as loudly as possible over a small lake. In fact, it was once recorded that someone's voice traveled 10½ miles across still water at night! Just think—if that were your mom calling, you'd have no excuse for not coming home on time.

Maybe you would like to see how fast you can talk. Find a favorite story and try reading it as fast as you can. Ready... Set... Go! Stop after a minute and count the number of words you have read. Did you beat the record of 650 words per minute, or did you get a bit "tongue-tied"?

Perhaps yodeling is something you'd like to try. It's a fun way to use your voice. Pretend you are on a mountain top. See how fast you can yodel. Chances are you would have a tough time beating the record of 22 tones in one second!

Possibly you enjoy rapping. A man in Chicago certainly does. He has a world record to prove it. In 54.9 seconds he was able to rap 674 syllables! That is most definitely a mouthful of sounds!

Next time an adult mentions that the noise you and your friends are making is becoming unbearable, share the above information. They may begin to think that children's noise is not so bad after all!

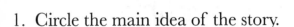

1. Circle the main idea of the story.

   Children really like to make noise.

   Some people like to set records by using their voices.

   Loud noise can damage your hearing.

2. Underline the true statements.

   Noise travels best in a noisy place.

   Most people probably read much slower than the world record holder.

   Yodeling probably takes practice.

3. Use the Word Bank to circle the words in the wordsearch related to making sound.

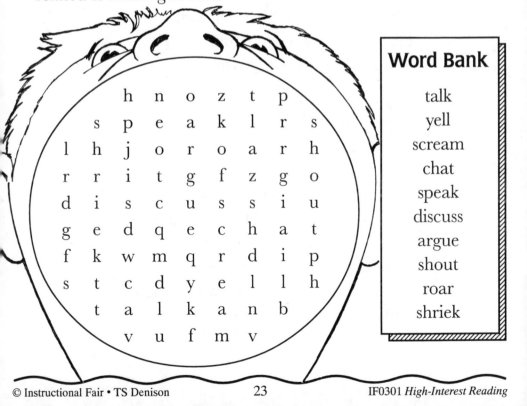

Word Bank

talk
yell
scream
chat
speak
discuss
argue
shout
roar
shriek

The Uninvited Arachnid

I lay upon my bed with ease,
Hoping to catch some peaceful "zs."
When suddenly to my surprise,
I felt a stare; I opened my eyes.
Eight long legs crawled over my feet,
Topped by a mouth that was eager to eat.
I could pull my spread up high
And cover each wide-opened eye,
Or take my pillow, flail about,
Jump on the bed, and loudly shout.
"Get outta here!" I would announce,
Eliminating its chance to pounce.
I will be brave! So with a heave,
I threw my pillow—felt relieved!
Then suddenly, it was gone.
I wouldn't be its little pawn.

I lay upon my bed with ease,
Hoping to catch some peaceful "zs."
When suddenly I realized
As I lay there immobilized,
I never saw the arachnid land!
"Where are you now? I do demand
To know if you're alive or dead
Or biding time upon my bed!"
This time, I pulled my spread up high
And covered each wide-opened eye.

Circle the correct answers.

1. **When** did the story probably take place?

      at night   at noon   mid-afternoon

2. **Who** was the uninvited guest?

      an octopus   a pillow   a spider

3. **Where** did the story occur?

      on a web   in bed   in a tree

4. **How** was the visitor asked to leave?

      with a note   by the butler   with a tossed pillow

5. **Why** did the speaker cover his/her eyes?

      Dust flew in them.   He/she was afraid.   He/she was playing a game.

Underline a word that has the same meaning as the boldface word.

1. Or take my pillow, **flail** about . . .

      fluff   sleep   beat

2. Eliminating its chance to **pounce**.

      jump   leave   eat

3. I wouldn't be his little **pawn**.

      hostage   criminal   friend

4. As I lay there **immobilized**,

      cold   motionless   frightened

5. Or **biding** time upon my bed!

      telling   waiting   looking

Snake Bites!

Snakes have been around since the beginning of time. Often people claim that they don't like snakes because they are wet and slimy. Actually, a snake's skin is dry, but it may appear slimy because of the way light bounces off its scales. These scales, which are really overlapping skin, provide protection from enemies and sharp rocks. A snake sheds its skin when it outgrows its old skin. This can occur twelve or more times a year! When people get sunburned, their skin flakes off. However, while we lose little bits and pieces of skin, a snake sheds all its skin at one time.

Some people think a snake's tail or its tongue is dangerous. This is not the case. For example, a rattlesnake's noisy tail actually warns an intruder of imminent danger. Its forked tongue is pointy and looks sharp, but it is actually very soft and is used to track its prey. Its fangs are really its deadly tools.

There are over 400 kinds of venomous snakes, whose fangs inject poison that is pumped from the snake's glands. Some of these have a bite that can be dangerous to humans. There are four deadly snakes that live in the United States. They are the moccasin, copperhead, coral snake, and rattlesnake.

Constrictors, such as boas and pythons, coil around their victims and suffocate them. These include some of the largest snakes in the world. One reticulated python measured over 32 feet in length.

Write **T** if a statement is true and **F** if it is false.

_____ Snakes can shed their skin more than once a year.

_____ A snake's tail can be very dangerous.

_____ Snakes are considered somewhat modern animals.

_____ A snake's scales are actually overlapping skin.

_____ A snake's skin is wet and slimy.

_____ A snake's forked tongue injects venom.

_____ Constrictors suffocate their victims.

_____ Snakes tear food apart with their fangs.

_____ Snakes shed their old skin a little at a time.

_____ There are over 400 deadly snakes that live in the United States.

_____ A rattlesnake's tail warns of danger.

_____ One of the largest snakes ever recorded measured over 32 feet long.

Just Between Friends

My dog Butch is my very best friend. He loves me, and I love him. We protect each other. He barks to warn me when my bossy neighbor Cassie is walking up the driveway. This gives me an excellent opportunity to hide upstairs in my closet. (She would never find me there. In fact, even I sometimes have trouble finding my way out of my messy closet!) To return the favor I warn Butch whenever Mom decides it's time for his bubble bath. That's when he and I go for a long hike in the nearby woods. We don't come home until we're sure Mom will say, "Where have you two been? Now we'll have to postpone Butch's bath for another day." Butch and I smile as we go upstairs and hope Mom will forget about it the next day.

There's something even more special about Butch. He's so smart that he can talk to me! I don't mean with the typical dog noises—grrrr, bowwow, and so on. I mean that he can actually utter words that I understand! Sometimes Butch and I will chat for hours. Other times we just say a few words because friends understand each other. I guess Mom and Dad probably think I'm talking to myself, but I'm really conversing with my best friend. No one knows about this except Butch and me—and now you. So please, keep it a secret!

Butch and I were also wondering if you know how to speak "Poodle." There's a cute little dog that he's dying to meet, but Butch is a little shy, so maybe you could introduce them.

1. Write a word from the story that means the same as the word in each bone above it.

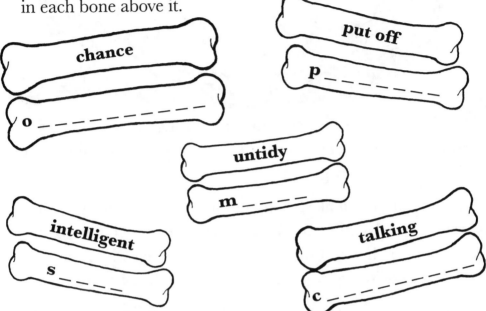

chance

o _ _ _ _ _ _ _ _

put off

p _ _ _ _ _ _ _ _

untidy

m _ _ _ _ _

intelligent

s _ _ _ _

talking

c _ _ _ _ _ _ _ _

2. Underline the lesson(s) that can be learned from the story.

It's great to have a best friend.

Dogs like to take baths.

Everyone should keep secrets—especially friends.

Some dogs can talk.

3. List three ways that tell how you and your best friend help each other.

a._____

b._____

c._____

Let's Dance!

Dancing has been *popular* from early through modern times. Almost anyone can learn to dance, and some people enjoy dancing every chance they get.

Laurie Churchwell likes to tap her toes so much that she tap danced almost 18 miles around a college *campus*! This amazing *feat* took her six hours. I wonder how her feet felt when she finished? A tub of warm water may have been their best reward.

Have you ever heard of the Chicken Dance? Some people in Cincinnati, Ohio, definitely have. About 48,000 residents joined in a Chicken Dance in 1994! *Imagine* all of the *squawking* and armflapping. No one felt "cooped up" on that record-setting day.

The people in China are famous for creating beautiful, dancing dragons. A long line of people *perform* under a huge dragon costume and dance through the streets of the city. What an *incredible* sight it must have been when 610 people lined up to form a dancing dragon that was 5,550 feet long! *Onlookers* must have been thankful that this giant dragon was not dangerous.

Now if you prefer speed in dancing versus performing with a large number of people, Stephen Gare's world record should interest you. He tap danced at a rate of 32 taps per second! How many times can you tap your toes in one second?

Use the Phrase Bank to write the correct phrases under each category.

Phrase Bank

involved 48,000 people

performed with a
    reptile costume

requires special shoes

squawk and flap arms

an 18-mile dance lasting
six hours

a famous dance in China

Tap Dance

_____

_____

Chicken Dance

_____

_____

Dragon Dance

_____

_____

2. Match the meaning to the italicized words in the story by writing the correct letter in the blanks.

_____ popular

_____ campus

_____ feat

_____ imagine

_____ squawking

_____ perform

_____ incredible

_____ onlookers

a. amazing

b. making loud noises

c. deed

d. to act

e. in demand

f. spectators

g. create in your mind

h. school grounds

A Sticky Solution

"Clean out your room! Pick up each shirt!
Use lots of soap! There's too much dirt!
If it's not cleaned, we both will know
Because of what will start to grow!"

I start to clean, and then I stop,
I first must finish my lollipop.
I bring it to my mouth to lick.
What's this stuff growing on the stick?
It's green, and furry, and not too sweet.
It's something I don't want to eat!
I put it down—sit on my bed
I feel the fur from my dog Fred.
The fur is fluffy—makes me sneeze
Perhaps because it's infested with fleas!
Slowly I peer way under my bed
That's where I keep some extra bread,
Peanut butter and jelly, too,
And lots of other things to chew.
Candy, gum, and cookies sweet
For when my tummy needs a treat.

I know my food's a little old,
But who replaced it with this mold?
And who invited all these ants?
What an ugly circumstance!
With one big sweep, I will deposit
All this garbage in the big hall closet!

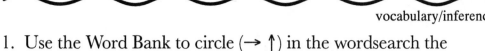

1. Use the Word Bank to circle (→ ↑) in the wordsearch the things found in the boy's room.

Word Bank

ants	candy	fleas	jelly	mold
bread	cookies	gum	lollipop	peanut butter

r	f	i	g	l	t	r	a	y	e	s	w
o	l	o	l	l	i	p	o	p	d	b	u
p	e	a	n	u	t	b	u	t	t	e	r
c	a	n	d	y	m	r	o	b	l	u	s
e	s	t	o	c	j	e	l	l	y	f	r
b	o	s	r	h	g	a	d	n	s	f	g
p	t	i	m	o	l	d	w	e	m	k	u
e	s	f	u	c	o	o	k	i	e	s	m

2. Place a check (✓) beside each true statement.

_____ The room hasn't been cleaned for a long time.

_____ The room's owner always follows his mom's instructions.

_____ The room's owner likes to clean.

_____ Mom will be happy with the results of his cleaning.

3. Circle what you predict will be the next place Mom will want cleaned.

the kitchen   the hall closet   the living room

Fantastic Felines

With its magnificent mane and muscular body, the lion is often referred to as the "king of beasts." Contrary to what most people believe, the lion is not the largest member of the cat family. That honor belongs to the tiger. It can be slightly larger than the lion.

Lions are the only big cats that live in groups (prides) which may contain as many as 30 members. The large male lion protects its pride's territory and also defends the females against other males. However, the male lion permits the females to do most of the hunting. The adult females surround their prey until they are ready to pounce. After their victim is killed, the male joins the other members to eat. One giraffe is enough to feed the entire pride. Other favorite prey are zebras and antelopes.

These same females that can be such mighty hunters also have a softer side. A lioness will give milk to any cub that seems hungry. Since all of the lionesses in the pride are related, she is actually feeding a young relative.

There is a greater difference in appearance between the male and female lions than between any other large male and female cats. What distinguishes the two lions is the male's huge, shaggy mane. Females have no mane. Also, male lions are much larger than females.

Match each word to its meaning by writing the letter on the line.

_____ magnificent   a. jump

_____ honor   b. group

_____ territory   c. space

_____ pride   d. wonderful

_____ pounce   e. special designation

Circle the correct answer about lions and write it on the line.

1. A _____ does most of the hunting.   female   male

2. A _____ leads the pride and   female   male
   defends its members.

3. A _____ joins the group after the   female   male
   hunting is completed.

4. A _____ does not have a mane.   female   male

5. A _____ is larger.   female   male

Write **T** if a statement is true, and **F** if it is false.

_____ 1. A tiger can be larger than a lion.

_____ 2. A lion usually hunts alone.

_____ 3. Antelopes and zebras are favorite foods of the lion.

_____ 4. One lion can devour an entire giraffe in one meal.

_____ 5. A pride may contain up to 100 lions.

The Bully Buster

Buster had become the target for the neighborhood bullies.

"Maybe one day you'll grow up and stand as tall as my knees!" yelled one tough-looking boy.

"You'd better run home quickly. I can hear your mom announcing that it's time for your nap!" smirked another.

Poor Buster was frustrated. Because he was so small, he was finding it difficult to make friends. The teasing was becoming unbearable. Feeling very melancholy, he kicked a rock and walked toward the park.

The park was empty. Buster sat down on a bench and began to daydream. "If only I could get some respect," he thought aloud. "Those guys would like me if they got to know me." When he bent down to pick up a stick, he quickly pulled back. What had appeared to be a thin stick was actually a tiny snake. Even more amazing, the snake began to speak.

"I've been observing you and listening to your problem, and I'll help you find a solution. Place me in your shirt pocket and we'll go visit those boys who are bothering you."

Buster did as the snake requested. He placed the tiny reptile in his shirt pocket and started off to find the bullies.

"Hey, look!" announced one of the boys. "Here comes the shrimp!"

When Buster approached them, something quite amazing happened. The snake grew very large as it slithered out of Buster's pocket. Quickly it surrounded the feet of the bullies who stood frozen in fear.

Answer Key

High-Interest Reading—Grade 3

Page 5

1. Read each statement. Write **F** if the statement is a **fact**— something that can be proved. Write **O** if the statement is an **opinion**—what someone believes.

   O The most difficult yo-yo trick is "Split the Atom."

   O Yo-yos created in Europe were very beautiful.

   F Philippine hunters developed a weapon they called a yo-yo.

   F Early Chinese yo-yos were made of ivory and silk cord.

   O Everyone enjoys playing with a yo-yo.

   F Donald Duncan's yo-yo was smaller than the Philippine version.

   O A person needs years of practice in order to perform difficult tricks using a yo-yo.

2. Fill in the circle that best describes the author's purpose in writing this article.

   ○ entertain   ● inform   ○ persuade

3. Check the box with the yo-yo that you would be most interested in trying. Then explain the reason why.

   ☐ the Chinese yo-yo   ☐ the Philippine yo-yo
   ☐ the European yo-yo   ☐ a modern yo-yo

   Why? *Answers will vary.*

Page 7

1. Circle the main idea of the story.
   - walking on stilts
   - hot-air balloons
   - (performing tricks high above the ground)

2. Draw a line from each person to his amazing feat.

   Col. Harry A. Froboess → performed a trapeze act while hanging from a hot-air balloon

   "Steady Eddy" Wolf → jumped into water from an airship

   Mike Howard → walked on very tall stilts

3. Answer the riddle by following the directions.

   Why did the diver choose to leap 100 feet down into a glass of soda pop?

   a. Cross out all words in the Word Bank that mean "amazing."

   b. Cross out all words that rhyme with "stilt."

   c. Write the remaining words from bottom to top.

Word Bank
~~astonishing~~
~~built~~
landings
easy
~~stunning~~
~~quilt~~
make
drinks
~~guilt~~
soft

   Soft drinks make easy landings.

Page 9

1. Number the events in the correct order.

   5 A strange visitor entered our tent.
   2 My friend and I talked and talked.
   1 Fuzz and I put up the tent.
   4 My teddy bear and I fell asleep.
   3 We fixed a delicious dinner.

2. On the line, write the letter of the meaning that matches each word or phrase.

   d "no time flat"   a. fall asleep
   b "grub"   b. food
   a "count sheep"   c. extra space
   e "prey"   d. quickly
   c "room to spare"   e. hunted animal(s)

3. Circle who you think we thought our visitor(s) might be.

   a. giant lions   c. angry gorillas   e. hungry cougars
   b. big bear   d. wild wolves

   Answers will vary.

   Find the animal words above in the puzzle and color those boxes **red**. Color the remaining boxes **black** to discover the name of

	B	I	G	B	E	A	R	
H	U	N	G	R	Y	C	O	U	G	A	R	S
G	I	A	N	T	L	I	O	N	S
A	N	G	R	Y	G	O	R	I	L	L	A	S
W	I	L	D	W	O	L	V	E	S

Page 11

Circle each correct answer.

1. An elephant is able to use its trunk in many different ways because its trunk . . .
   - is very long.
   - is a combination of its nose and upper lip.
   - (contains over 100,000 muscles.)

2. The result of an elephant walking on its tiptoes means that the elephant can . . .
   - almost reach the height of a giraffe.
   - (walk very quietly.)
   - climb over large rocks easily.

3. Because an elephant rolls in muddy water it . . .
   - (can appear to be a different color.)
   - needs to bathe often.
   - is shunned by other animals.

Write each phrase in the correct category.

Phrase Bank	
usually only males have tusks	have larger ears
are used more often in circuses	are heavier and taller

African Elephants
1. *are heavier + taller*
2. *have larger ears*

Asian Elephants
1. *more often in circuses*
2. *only males have tusks*

Page 13

1. Use six different colors. Color each pair of spots the same color if the word and phrase mean the same.

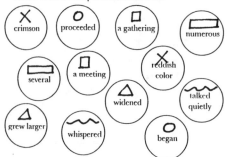

2. Underline the statements that are true about this story.

   <u>Susie's trick backfired.</u>

   Susie didn't have to go to school only because her mother thought she had the chicken pox.

   Susie fooled her neighbor.

   <u>Susie wasn't happy with the results of her trick.</u>

3. Predict what Susie will do for the rest of the day.

   Answers will vary.

Page 15

1. Write **F** on the blank if the statement is a fact. Write **O** if the statement is an opinion.

   O Long hair is very becoming.

   F In the article, the longest beard measured longer than the widest mustache.

   O People are very proud of their hair.

   O A long mustache is silly.

   F Human hair is much thinner than a pencil.

   O Short hair is easier to take care of.

   O People with long hair live longer.

   O Men with long hair are more handsome.

Circle the correct answer.

2. What do all of the people in the story have in common?

   very long hair

   (setting world records for hair growth)

   lots of ways to style hair

3. Draw a line to match each person with the gift best suited for him or her.

   Hans N. Langseth —— mustache wax

   Mata Jagdamba —— bib

   Kalyan Ramji Sain —— barrettes

Page 17

1. Circle the main idea of this poem.

   climbing a tall tower

   climbing a mountain

   (climbing up to the top bunk)

2. Draw a line from each word to its meaning.

   physique —— go upward

   peak —— very easy

   elevate —— strength

   "a piece of cake" —— body structure

   force —— top of hill or mountain

3. Climb the ladder by reading each clue. Then unscramble and write the word from the poem on each step.

	Clues
tower (eowrt)	a tall building
breathe (tbherae)	to move air in and out of the mouth
muscles (lcemuss)	body tissue that moves bones
problem (rlompbe)	something that needs to be solved
nonsense (soneenns)	a silly thought

Page 19

1. Define each italicized word from the story by writing the letter of its meaning on the blank.

   d cub   a. grinding teeth

   j den   b. spend the winter in dormant state

   i carnivore   c. hairless

   f dine   d. baby bear

   b hibernate   e. unable to see

   c bald   f. eat

   e blind   g. unprotected

   a molars   h. go to sleep

   h retire   i. meat-eater

   g defenseless j. cave

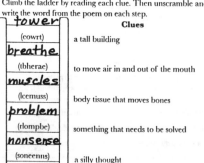

2. List one food each type of bear enjoys.

   Brown Bear   Panda   Polar Bear

   berries,   bamboo   seals
   fish, roots

3. List three changes that occur as a bear grows older.

   a. can see

   b. grows hair

   c. grows larger

Page 21

Circle the correct answer(s) to each question.

1. What lesson did the speaker in the story learn?

   (Make the best you can of a situation.)

   Do not throw stones or you may hit something.

   Rabbits are magical creatures.

2. What clues indicate how the speaker was changing?

   He found a rabbit's foot.

   (His feet grew very large and were covered with fur.)

   (Whiskers sprouted from his face.)

   He was standing in a field of clover.

3. How do you know that the speaker was not too upset?

   He went to sleep.

   (He decided to accept the situation.)

   His whole body tingled.

Cross out the word in each row that doesn't mean the same as the others.

a. entertain   amuse   ~~work~~

b. ~~happy~~   weary   disheartened

c. discovered   ~~lost~~   found

d. stroked   rubbed   ~~carried~~

e. ~~enormous~~   situation   circumstance

Page 23

1. Circle the main idea of the story.

   Children really like to make noise.

   (Some people like to set records by using their voices.)

   Loud noise can damage your hearing.

2. Underline the true statements.

   Noise travels best in a noisy place.

   Most people probably read much slower than the world record holder.

   Yodeling probably takes practice.

3. Use the Word Bank to circle the words in the wordsearch related to making sound.

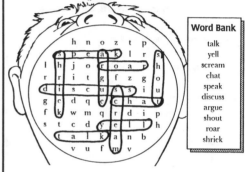

Word Bank

talk
yell
scream
chat
speak
discuss
argue
shout
roar
shrick

Page 25

1. at night   2. a spider   3. in bed
4. with a tossed pillow   5. He/she was afraid
1. beat   2. jump   3. hostage   4. motionless
5. waiting

Page 27

__I__ Snakes can shed their skin more than once a year.

__F__ A snake's tail can be very dangerous.

__F__ Snakes are considered somewhat modern animals.

__I__ A snake's scales are actually overlapping skin.

__F__ A snake's skin is wet and slimy.

__F__ A snake's forked tongue injects venom.

__I__ Constrictors suffocate their victims.

__F__ Snakes tear food apart with their fangs.

__F__ Snakes shed their old skin a little at a time.

__F__ There are over 400 deadly snakes that live in the United States.

__T__ A rattlesnake's tail warns of danger.

__I__ One of the largest snakes ever recorded measured over 32 feet long.

Page 29

1. Write a word from the story that means the same as the word in each bone above it.

2. Underline the lesson(s) that can be learned from the story.

   It's great to have a best friend.

   Dogs like to take baths.

   Everyone should keep secrets—especially friends.

   Some dogs can talk.

3. List three ways that tell how you and your best friend help each other.

   a. _Answers will vary._

   b._____

   c._____

Page 31

Use the Phrase Bank to write the correct phrases under each category.

Phrase Bank

involved 48,000 people	squawk and flap arms
performed with a	an 18-mile dance lasting
reptile costume	six hours
requires special shoes	a famous dance in China

Tap Dance
requires special shoes
18-mile dance lasting 6 hours

Chicken Dance
48,000 people
squawk + flap arms

Dragon Dance
famous dance in China
uses reptile costume

2. Match the meaning to the italicized words in the story by writing the correct letter in the blanks.

_e_ popular   a. amazing
_h_ campus   b. making loud noises
_c_ feat   c. deed
_g_ imagine   d. to act
_b_ squawking   e. in demand
_d_ perform   f. spectators
_a_ incredible   g. create in your mind
_f_ onlookers   h. school grounds

Page 33

1. Use the Word Bank to circle (→ ↑) in the wordsearch the things found in the boy's room.

Word Bank

ants	candy	fleas	jelly	mold
bread	cookies	gum	lollipop	peanut butter

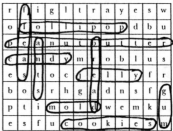

2. Place a check (✓) beside each true statement.

_✓_ The room hasn't been cleaned for a long time.
____ The room's owner always follows his mom's instructions.
____ The room's owner likes to clean.
____ Mom will be happy with the results of his cleaning.

3. Circle what you predict will be the next place Mom will want cleaned.

the kitchen   (the hall closet)   the living room

Page 35

Match each word to its meaning by writing the letter on the line.

_d_ magnificent   a. jump
_e_ honor   b. group
_c_ territory   c. space
_b_ pride   d. wonderful
_a_ pounce   e. special designation

Circle the correct answer about lions and write it on the line.

1. A _female_ does most of the hunting. (female) male
2. A _male_ leads the pride and defends its members. female (male)
3. A _male_ joins the group after the hunting is completed. female (male)
4. A _female_ does not have a mane. (female) male
5. A _male_ is larger. female (male)

Write **T** if a statement is true, and **F** if it is false.

_T_ 1. A tiger can be larger than a lion.
_F_ 2. A lion usually hunts alone.
_T_ 3. Antelopes and zebras are favorite foods of the lion.
_F_ 4. One lion can devour an entire giraffe in one meal.
_F_ 5. A pride may contain up to 100 lions.

Page 37

4 6 3 5 1 2
Answers will vary.

Page 39

Blowing Bubble Gum
1. _gum_
2. _chew_

Making Soap Bubbles
1. _soap_
2. _wand_

Creating a Balloon Sculpture
1. _rubber_
2. _art_

2. Cross out the word/phrase in each row that does not belong.

a. famous   well-known   ~~unknown~~
b. ~~certainly~~   perhaps   maybe
c. inflate   ~~deflate~~   fill with air
d. ~~capture~~   release   free
e. reproduction   copy   ~~original~~

Page 41

Circle the sentences that are true.

1. How does a giraffe benefit by being tall?

   (It can reach the leaves on the tops of the trees.)

   (It can observe its enemies from far away.)

   The air is cooler up high.

2. What are the disadvantages to being tall?

   (It is difficult to eat leaves on small trees or bushes.)

   (It could be more difficult to hide.)

   (It is difficult to drink water from a watering hole.)

Circle all the corresponding words that have similar meanings.

1. **tall**

   (high)   (lanky)   rear   (towering)   tattle

2. **approaching**

   leaving   (nearing)   carrying   (advancing)   dropping

3. **observe**

   (notice)   cover   (examine)   help   (watch)

4. **sharp**

   outline   flat   (pointy)   clean   wide

5. **generally**

   (normally)   hardly   (usually)   (commonly)   easily

6. **hindrance**

   support   (prevention)   (obstruction)   (problem)

Page 43

1. Circle the main idea of this poem.

   (Groups of words often mean something very different)

   • The speaker's parents sometimes act very silly.

   • The speaker's parents have trouble understanding each other.

2. Write the letter of the corresponding meaning on the blank line beside each idiom.

   f "eats like a bird"   a. You make me feel happy.

   d "a square meal"   b. playing a card game

   a "you light up my life!"   c. Make your money last.

   b "playing bridge"   d. a well-balanced meal

   c "Stretch your money."   e. a heavy rainstorm

   g "a fork in the road"   f. light eater

   e "It's raining cats and dogs." g. the road turns in different directions.

Think hard!

Suppose you promised Mom that by tomorrow morning you would: clean your bedroom, complete a book report, practice the piano, study your spelling words, and help wash the car. Mom says, "Don't bite off more than you can chew!"

What does she mean? *Don't promise to do more than is possible.*

Page 45

Read each statement. Check the set of boxes on the left to indicate whether you agree or disagree with the statement. Then **after** reading the article check the set of boxes on the right to see if you still feel the same way about each statement.

Before Reading			After Reading	
Agree	Disagree		Agree	Disagree
☐	☐	Gorillas and humans have very similar diets.	☐	☑
☐	☐	Gorillas prefer living atop tall trees.	☐	☑
☐	☐	Humans are gorillas' worst enemies.	☑	☐
☐	☐	A gorilla prefers to live with other gorillas rather than alone.	☑	☐

Answers will vary.

Use context clues to define each italicized word from the story. Write the letter of its meaning on the line.

d threatening   a. eat; chew and swallow

f predominant   b. share information; relay messages

a consume   c. predicament; situation

b communicate   d. menacing; dangerous

e poachers   e. illegal hunters

c plight   f. one who holds authority over others

Page 47

1. Use six different-colored crayons. Color a word on a spoke in the first tire the same color as a word with a similar meaning on the second tire.

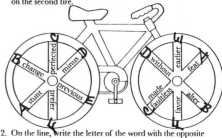

2. On the line, write the letter of the word with the opposite meaning.

   c young   a. remain

   d larger   b. pull

   e minus   c. old

   b push   d. smaller

   a change   e. plus

3. Circle the main idea of the story.

   Everyone can ride a bike.

   (There are some amazing bikes and tricks.)

   Children like bicycling.

Page 49

1. Number the events in the correct order.

   2 Friends decide to go skating.
   3 He/she searches for the skates.
   6 He/she discovers they're going roller skating.
   1 The phone rings.
   4 He/she dresses in warm clothing.
   5 Friend is waiting at the door.

2. Write each word or group of words in the correct column.

   Word Bank

roll	wheels	glide and slide
icy surface	wooden or paved surface	blades

Roller Skating	Ice Skating
roll	blades
wheels	glide + slide
wood/paved surface	icy surface

3. Circle the best answer.

   So misunderstandings don't occur in the future, the speaker should . . .

   clean his/her room very thoroughly.

   (listen very carefully when plans are being made.)

   give his/her dog something better to chew.

Page 51

1. Check each characteristic of the kangaroo that is true. The kangaroo . . .

   ____ is a meat-eater.
   ✓ can eat while hopping.
   ✓ has very large hind feet.
   ✓ protects its baby in its pouch.
   ✓ has extremely powerful back legs.
   ____ gives birth to very large babies.
   ✓ uses its long tail for balance.
   ____ usually lives in Australia and New Mexico.

2. Cross off the word in each row that doesn't belong. Then use the Word Bank to write a word that does belong in the group.

Word Bank	drop	framework	notice	seize
	empower	linger	permit	wonderful

   1. ~~design~~ board construction **framework**
   2. ~~pick~~ grab snatch **seize**
   3. ~~see~~ observe watch **notice**
   4. let ~~cancel~~ allow **permit**
   5. enable authorize ~~strong~~ **empower**
   6. ~~common~~ fantastic amazing **wonderful**
   7. tumble fall ~~thimble~~ **drop**
   8. ~~reply~~ remain stay **linger**

Page 53

Circle the correct answer.

1. **When** did the story take place?

   in the spring   (on a windy day)   during the morning

2. **Who** had just celebrated a birthday?

   Grandfather   (Dion)   Mother

3. **What** was the birthday present?

   a long trip   a sandbox   (a kite)

4. **Who** had given the present?

   (Grandfather)   a friend   Mother

5. **Why** was the kite so special?

   It was very large.   (It could make its owner fly.)
   It flew over hills.

Draw one long kite tail from each word to its meaning.

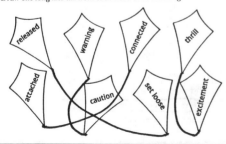

Page 55

1. Circle the main idea of the poem.

   reading a calendar   different hairstyles
   (not wanting a haircut)

2. Circle all the correct answers.

   You can guess that the speaker probably . . .

   (exaggerates.)   (dislikes haircuts.)   wants to become a barber.
   has long hair.   (is glad it's the puppy's turn for a haircut.)

3. Use the clues to complete the crossword puzzle.

   Across
   2. an opposite of shrink
   4. to use a lot of
   8. a great work of art
   9. hairless

   Down
   1. to delay
   3. to plead
   5. to tremble
   6. oily matter
   7. to cry loudly

Crossword answers: grow, slather, masterpiece, bald, postpone, beg, grease, shiver

Page 57

1. Circle the correct animal in each sentence.

   a. When (An alligator / a crocodile) [*An alligator* circled] clamps down its jaws, no lower teeth are visible.

   b. (An alligator's / A crocodile's) [*A crocodile's* circled] head is more massive although it is more tapered.

   c. (An alligator / A crocodile) [*A crocodile* circled] absorbs the sun's heat through its open mouth to convert into energy for later activities.

   d. (An alligator / A crocodile) [*A crocodile* circled] moves swiftly in water and on land.

2. Complete each statement by circling the correct answer.

   a. Because a crocodile is carnivorous…
      - (it eats animals like fish and frogs.) [circled]
      - it must drag its food in the water before chewing.

   b. Because a crocodile often imitates an old, floating log…
      - it can remain afloat undisturbed for long periods of time.
      - (it can surprise its unsuspecting prey.) [circled]

   c. Because a crocodile remains still in the sun with an open mouth…
      - (it is known for its crocodile smile.) [circled]
      - it catches insects.

Page 59

Circle each correct answer.

1. In the poem how many children had watched the rain?
   one   (two)   several

2. Mom's instructions were: "Don't get . . . _____!"
   wet   silly   (muddy)

3. Everything went dark when . . .
   (the speaker was hit by a mudball.) [circled]
   the lights went out in the storm.
   the speaker dropped his glasses.

4. What are "mounds and mounds?"
   drops   balls   (heaps)

5. What clue helped Mom realize what her children had done?
   muddy shoe prints   (muddy footprints)   a pile of dirty clothes

6. Match the two words that have similar meanings by writing the corresponding letter in the blank.

   e darted   a. collecting
   b discuss   b. talk
   d frozen   c. desire
   f secret   d. motionless
   c want   e. dashed
   a gathering   f. hidden

Page 61

1. Write two ways in which Murphy and Oogo were the same and two ways in which they were different.

   Same
   a. Wanted to run away
   b. both had parents

   Different
   a. came from different planets
   b. looked different

2. Explain what Murphy meant when he said: "There's no place like home."

   Sugg. Answer: Your home is a very special place.

3. Circle the main idea in the story.
   Murphy wanted to run away from home.
   (Murphy and Oogo were both different, yet similar.) [circled]
   Children should do all of their chores and listen to their parents.

Page 63

Circle the correct answers.

1. Which traits describe a whale?
   (intelligent)   clumsy   (gentle)   slow-witted
   (graceful)   (enormous)   (warm-blooded)   rough skin

2. What is the purpose of blubber?
   It adds to the beauty of the whale.
   (It keeps the whale warm.) [circled]
   It helps a whale use its spout.

Use words from the story and the clues to complete the crossword puzzle.

Across
2. very large water mammals
5. takes in air
6. gigantic
7. non-violent; calm

Down
1. a tool used to measure weight
3. top of the water
4. written down
6. died out

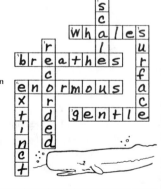

Crossword answers:
- 2 Across: Whales
- 5 Across: breathes
- 6 Across: enormous
- 7 Across: gentle
- Down: scale / surface / record / extinct

Page 65

1. Explain this statement: "Sticks and stones may break my bones but names will never hurt me!"

   Sugg. Answer: Objects can hurt me, but name-calling cannot.

   Do you agree? _____ Why or why not? _____
   Answers will vary.

2. Complete this "nice word" puzzle with words from the Word Bank.

   Word Bank
   admire
   appreciate
   compliment
   encourage
   love
   share

   Crossword:
   ```
           a       l
           p       o
   c o m P l i m E n t
           r       v
           e       E
     e n c o u r a g e
           i
           A d m i r e
           t
     s h a r E
   ```

Page 67

Use each clue to fill in the blank with the correct word.

a. _April Scott_ (who) owns an enormous rag _doll_ (what). It is almost 42 _feet_ (what) tall.

b. Jigsaw _puzzles_ (what) can be difficult to do, especially when the people in _France_ (where) create one. Theirs had almost 44,000 _pieces_ (what).

c. A gum-wrapper _chain_ (what) can be fun to make. All that you need to do is chew lots of _gum_ (what), save the _wrappers_ (what), and fold them together.

d. On a snowy day it can be fun to build a _snowman_ (what). The more _snow_ (what) that you use, the bigger it will become. Some people in _Japan_ (where) used lots of _snow_ (what) to create a very, very large _snowman_ (what).

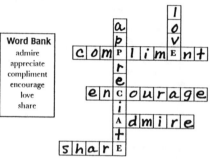

Page 69

Fill in the circle beside the correct answer(s).

1. This story is . . .
   ○ factual.
   ● fiction.

2. What statement supports your first answer?
   ○ Some boys do make messes.
   ● Monster Mess-Makers do not exist.
   ○ Parents want their children to be neat.

3. Which details describe the mess in the kitchen?
   ● gobs of peanut butter and grape jelly
   ○ pointy, yellow teeth
   ● a huge puddle of spilled milk
   ○ eyes that glow bright orange
   ○ tiny footsteps

4. In which situation(s) would Tommy's Monster Mess-Maker return?
   ○ a neat and tidy chest of drawers
   ● melting ice cream dripping on the counter
   ● paint spilling from a can on the basement floor
   ● a tipped-over bowl of popcorn
   ○ a well-made bed
   ● clothes thrown on the closet floor

Page 71

1. Cross off the word/phrase in each list that does not belong.

   a. envision   imagine   ~~wear glasses~~
   b. raised designs   embossed   ~~be in charge~~
   c. ~~go in reverse~~   progressed   advanced
   d. intrigue   ~~not related~~   arouse curiosity
   e. ~~cities~~   enthusiasts   people who show interest

2. List three reasons why you think Frisbees were eventually made from plastic rather than the original metal. _Sugg. Answers._
   Flew better
   Cheaper
   Kept its shape better
   More colorful

3. How would you modify (change) the Frisbee's construction to make it better? Why?
   Answers will vary.

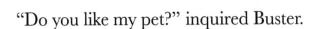

"Do you like my pet?" inquired Buster.

"Uhhh, sure!" they squeaked, still motionless.

"Maybe we can play together later today," suggested Buster.

"Whatever you say," they answered.

Suddenly the snake shriveled up and returned to its original size. Once again, Buster tucked it inside his pocket. "See you later," he said as he returned to the park.

Number the events below in the correct order.

_____ The snake began to talk.

_____ The bullies stood frozen in fear.

_____ Buster spied a twig on the ground.

_____ The snake grew very large.

_____ The bullies tease Buster.

_____ Buster walks to the park.

Predict what happened when Buster and the snake returned to the park.

_____

_____

_____

_____

All Puffed Up

Fill your cheeks with air and puff them up. Inflate them as large as possible. Now release the air. Maybe you, too, can become a world record holder. "How?" you ask. Read further, and you should get some ideas.

If you like to chew gum, this may be something you would like to try. Be sure to use a lot of bubble-gum and chew, chew, chew. If you practice long enough, you may blow a bubble larger than the one created by Susan Williams. She blew a bubble-gum bubble with a diameter of nearly 2 feet! Let's hope someone didn't decide to pop it while it was still in her mouth.

Perhaps bubble-gum blowing isn't your thing. Maybe inflating balloons interests you more. Be creative and use the balloons to form something interesting. Some students in the Netherlands used their skills to combine both their lung capacity and their hand dexterity to create a reproduction of a famous VanGogh painting. They used 25,344 inflated, colorful balloons to create the illusion of fishing boats on a beach.

Maybe you would prefer forming a huge soap bubble as Alan McKay did. He used a super bubble wand, dishwashing liquid, glycerine, and water to form a bubble that was nearly 64 feet long!

Do you have enough bubble ideas now? Take a deep breath or get some soap bubbles and practice, practice, practice!

1. Use the Word Bank to write each related word in the correct bubble.

Word Bank

rubber	gum	chew
art	soap	wand

Blowing Bubble Gum

1. _____

2. _____

Making Soap Bubbles

1. _____

2. _____

Creating a Balloon Sculpture

1. _____

2. _____

2. Cross out the word/phrase in each row that does not belong.

a. famous   well-known   unknown

b. certainly   perhaps   maybe

c. inflate   deflate   fill with air

d. capture   release   free

e. reproduction   copy   original

Gentle Giants

Giraffes certainly do not need to be told to stand up straight and tall. One giraffe was almost 20 feet tall! A giraffe's height is attained by its very long, thin legs and its very, very long neck. This helps a giraffe easily observe approaching enemies such as lions and leopards. Because a giraffe prefers not to fight, it will run from an enemy that comes too close. But when necessary, a giraffe will kick with its long legs and sharp feet. Sometimes it will even use its long, strong neck to hit its enemy.

Believe it or not, a giraffe's size can also help him hide. While it feeds on tall trees, it can sometimes camouflage itself by appearing to be a tree. This occurs when the giraffe remains very still.

A giraffe's long legs can also be a hindrance. Bending down for water is difficult. A giraffe cannot kneel so it must spread its legs, in stiff, clumsy jerks, far apart. This prevents it from running and fighting if an enemy appears. At times like this, a giraffe might envy the shorter animals nearby.

Yet another interesting feature of the giraffe is its long tail. The giraffe uses the long coarse hairs on the end like a fly-swatter to flick away flies and other insects that disturb this gentle giant.

Circle the sentences that are true.

1. How does a giraffe benefit by being tall?

   It can reach the leaves on the tops of the trees.

   It can observe its enemies from far away.

   The air is cooler up high.

2. What are the disadvantages to being tall?

   It is difficult to eat leaves on small trees or bushes.

   It could be more difficult to hide.

   It is difficult to drink water from a watering hole.

Circle all the corresponding words that have similar meanings.

1. **tall**

   high   lanky   rear   towering   tattle

2. **approaching**

   leaving   nearing   carrying   advancing   dropping

3. **observe**

   notice   cover   examine   help   watch

4. **sharp**

   outline   flat   pointy   clean   wide

5. **generally**

   normally   hardly   usually   commonly   easily

6. **hindrance**

   support   prevention   obstruction   problem

Parent Talk

Dad rides on his bike but doesn't go anywhere.

His food is on a round plate, but he calls his meal "square."

Mom eats like a bird, but a bird eats a lot.

When she says she's full, her stomach's tied in knots.

Sometimes they play bridge with their friends at the table.

There's no water below! I don't see how they're able.

"You light up my life!" Dad tells Mom, and they kiss,

But I surely don't see any "on/off" switch.

"There's a fork in the road," they'll announce, "up ahead."

With no knife or no spoon, they must be misled.

"It's raining cats and dogs!" I hear them proclaim.

I see only water. Pets are not to blame.

Mom teaches a lesson: "Stretch all of your money."

Money's paper or metal so that really sounds funny!

"You're such a sweet dear," they always tell me.

Have I grown pointed antlers that only they see?

"Cute as a button!" I remember Mom said.

Do I have holes in my face? Does thread grow from my head?

It's hard to communicate with parents—It's true,

But, do they understand each other? Do **they** have a clue?

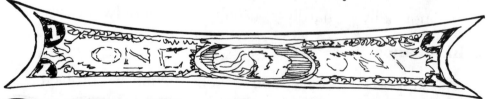

1. Circle the main idea of this poem.

   • Groups of words often mean something very different.

   • The speaker's parents sometimes act very silly.

   • The speaker's parents have trouble understanding each other.

2. Write the letter of the corresponding meaning on the blank line beside each idiom.

   ____ "eats like a bird"   a. You make me feel happy.

   ____ "a square meal"   b. playing a card game

   ____ "You light up my life!"   c. Make your money last.

   ____ "playing bridge"   d. a well-balanced meal

   ____ "Stretch your money."   e. a heavy rainstorm

   ____ "a fork in the road"   f. light eater

   ____ "It's raining cats and dogs." g. The road turns in different directions.

Think hard!

Suppose you promised Mom that by tomorrow morning you would: clean your bedroom, complete a book report, practice the piano, study your spelling words, and help wash the car. Mom says, "Don't bite off more than you can chew!"

What does she mean? _____

_____

_____

Ape Over Gorillas

Before reading this article, go to page 45 and follow the directions for the prereading exercise.

Although adult gorillas can stand 5½ to 6 feet tall and appear to be very *threatening*, these creatures are actually slow-moving, gentle, and peaceful unless they are disturbed. Usually they enjoy resting and eating the leaves, stems, and shoots of plants.

Gorillas live in groups that contain between five and ten members. Generally, there is one *predominant* male, several females, and their young.

Although they can climb, gorillas spend their lives mostly on the ground. When they travel far, they "knuckle-walk," that is, they move on all fours with their weight resting on the middle joints of their fingers.

Gorillas' dinners are quite simple. In the mountains they tend to eat small trees, bamboo shoots, and tall herbs. In the lowlands they *consume* lots of fruit—especially woody fruits.

Gorillas in captivity have demonstrated high intelligence. Their ability to *communicate* is amazing. They become close to their trainers and sometimes other animals. They can even be taught sign language.

The gorilla's worst enemy is man. *Poachers* kill gorillas for money, and loggers cut down the trees they need for food. In recent years books and movies have been written about gorillas to make people aware of their *plight*. Unless care is taken to protect them, these gentle giants could disappear.

Read each statement. Check the set of boxes on the left to indicate whether you agree or disagree with the statement. Then **after** reading the article, check the set of boxes on the right to see if you still feel the same way about each statement.

Before Reading			*After Reading*	
Agree	**Disagree**		**Agree**	**Disagree**
☐	☐	Gorillas and humans have very similar diets.	☐	☐
☐	☐	Gorillas prefer living atop tall trees.	☐	☐
☐	☐	Humans are gorillas' worst enemies.	☐	☐
☐	☐	A gorilla prefers to live with other gorillas rather than alone.	☐	☐

Use context clues to define each italicized word from the story. Write the letter of its meaning on the line.

_____ threatening a. eat; chew and swallow

_____ predominant b. share information; relay messages

_____ consume c. predicament; situation

_____ communicate d. menacing; dangerous

_____ poachers e. illegal hunters

_____ plight f. one who holds authority over others

A Bicycle Built for Who?

When you were very young, you may have ridden a push cart and scooted with your legs. As you grew older, you probably switched to a tricycle. Then came a bicycle with training wheels, followed by a bike minus the training wheels. So now do you think you've come to the top of the cycling sport and perfected the art of riding on wheels? Read further, and you may change your mind.

First, get a ruler, a pencil, and some paper. Draw a line 3/4" long. Now draw a circle around the line. Then make another circle about the same size nearby. Hmmmm—What does this represent? Neville Patten from Australia rode a bicycle with tires the size of the circles you just drew for a distance of over 13 feet!

Was the previous bicycle a little small for you? Maybe you would like to try something larger. Use your imagination to picture a bicycle with tires that are 10 feet in diameter. Steve Gordon rode such a bike! That vehicle stood over 11 feet high.

Perhaps you consider yourself more of a stunt rider. Rather than let the size of a bike influence you, you prefer doing stunts on your bicycle—such as "popping a wheelie." Then maybe you are just the person to challenge Leandro Basseto, who rode on only one tire for almost 11 hours!

Whatever your preference in bike riding, remember to ride safely. Use a helmet, make sure your bike is in good working contion, signal when turning, and watch out for traffic!

1. Use six different-colored crayons. Color a word on a spoke in the first tire the same color as a word with a similar meaning on the second tire.

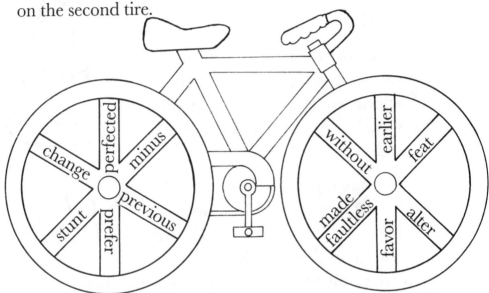

change   perfected   minus   previous   stunt   prefer

without   earlier   feat   made   faultless   favor   alter

2. On the line, write the letter of the word with the opposite meaning.

_____ young   a. remain

_____ larger   b. pull

_____ minus   c. old

_____ push   d. smaller

_____ change   e. plus

3. Circle the main idea of the story.

    Everyone can ride a bike.

    There are some amazing bikes and tricks.

    Children like bicycling.

The Skating Lesson

R-r-r-ring!

I would love to go! Let's meet at four.
I will be standing at my front door.
It's been awhile since I've been skating.
It sounds like fun—I'll be waiting.
Good-bye!

Where are my skates? Where do they lie?
Why is this room such a pig sty?
Where did I put them… in a drawer
In the closet… on the floor?
Are they under my bed—no, they're not there.
I remember! They're in the old shed.
They're safe away from my dog Lou.
All he does is chew, chew, chew!

Whew!
Found them! Now what else do I need?
A warm coat, my scarf, and mittens, indeed!

I'm bundled up, and it's time to go.
I hope they've shoveled off all the snow!

Ding-dong!
Hi. I'm ready! I have been waiting.
What? You mean we're going **roller** skating?

1. Number the events in the correct order.

_____ Friends decide to go skating.

_____ He/she searches for the skates.

_____ He/she discovers they're going roller skating.

_____ The phone rings.

_____ He/she dresses in warm clothing.

_____ Friend is waiting at the door.

2. Write each word or group of words in the correct column.

Word Bank		
roll	wheels	glide and slide
icy surface	wooden or paved surface	blades

Roller Skating   **Ice Skating**

_____   _____

_____   _____

_____   _____

3. Circle the best answer.

So misunderstandings don't occur in the future, the speaker should . . .

clean his/her room very thoroughly.

listen very carefully when plans are being made.

give his/her dog something better to chew.

Big Foot

If you observe a kangaroo, you will notice that its hind legs and feet are very large. With the help of its large tail for balance, the legs enable the kangaroo to hop very fast (over 30 mph). Although its legs are strong, their design does not allow them to walk as we do. The kangaroo is unable to move each back leg independently unless it is swimming.

There are about 50 different kinds of kangaroos in Australia and New Guinea. All kangaroos are herbivores. Sometimes they snatch a plant and eat "on the run"; other times they graze like cattle, remaining in one place for a period of time.

An amazing feature of the female kangaroo is her deep pouch that opens forward. A joey must climb up to the opening and tumble down inside in order to get its mother's milk. A newborn joey weighs only about 1/30 ounce, is blind, and has no hair. Even after it is older and can move by itself, the young joey sleeps, travels, and stays away from danger by hiding in its mother's pouch.

1. Check each characteristic of the kangaroo that is true.
   The kangaroo . . .

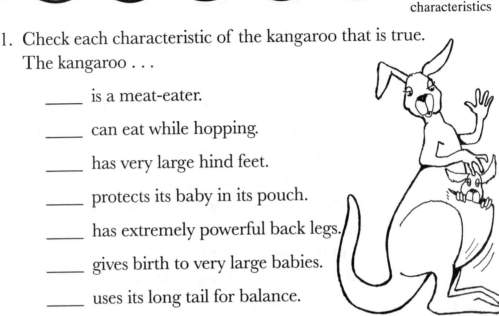

   _____ is a meat-eater.

   _____ can eat while hopping.

   _____ has very large hind feet.

   _____ protects its baby in its pouch.

   _____ has extremely powerful back legs.

   _____ gives birth to very large babies.

   _____ uses its long tail for balance.

   _____ usually lives in Australia and New Mexico.

2. Cross off the word in each row that doesn't belong. Then use
   the Word Bank to write a word that does belong in the group.

Word Bank	drop	framework	notice	seize
	empower	linger	permit	wonderful

1. design   board   construction _____

2. give   grab   snatch   _____

3. try   observe   watch   _____

4. let   cancel   allow   _____

5. enable   authorize strong   _____

6. common   fantastic amazing   _____

7. tumble   fall   thimble   _____

8. replay   remain   stay   _____

A Wild Ride

Dion had just received a new kite for his birthday. Imagine his excitement when the wind began to blow. "Mom, I'm going outside to try my new kite," he announced as he raced out the door.

"Let's see," Dion mumbled to himself. "Everything seems to be okay. I've attached a long, colorful tail and a huge ball of string, and now I'm ready for action!" So Dion raced down the field as he released the kite. His eyes followed closely as the kite seemed to perform for him in the blue sky. It dove down low and shot up rapidly as it formed loops while chasing after a cloud.

Suddenly the wind changed directions and became much stronger. Dion could barely keep a grip on the handles of the string. Then suddenly, his feet were lifted off the ground. He began to rise above the trees!

"Wheee!" exclaimed Dion, although he was a bit surprised. Then he remembered what his grandfather had said when he gave Dion the kite, "Treat the kite kindly, Dion, and you will have great adventures!" Those special instructions rang in his head as he flew over his house and saw his little brother playing in the sandbox.

"Super!" Dion announced as he glided above his school, past the park, and over his grandfather's house. Down below, his grandfather waved proudly to his airborne grandson.

Dion retraced his route. As he again flew over his house, the wind began to die down, and he slowly floated to the ground.

"How's the new kite?" his mother asked.

"Very, very special!" Dion answered, grinning from ear to ear.

Circle the correct answer.

1. **When** did the story take place?

    in the spring   on a windy day   during the morning

2. **Who** had just celebrated a birthday?

    Grandfather   Dion   Mother

3. **What** was the birthday present?

    a long trip   a sandbox   a kite

4. **Who** had given the present?

    Grandfather   a friend   Mother

5. **Why** was the kite so special?

    It was very large.   It could make its owner fly.

    It flew over hills.

Draw one long kite tail from each word to its meaning.

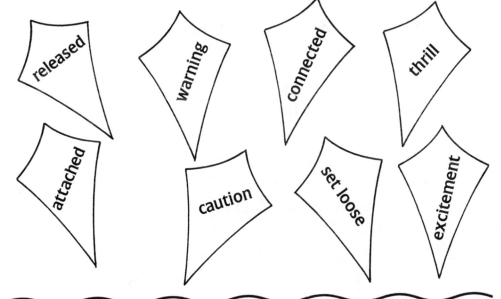

Hair Scare

"Haircut!" the calendar says today.
A word like that turns my hair gray!
Okay, I know it's time to go,
But my hair's finally begun to grow!
Last time, my head was almost bald.
You should have heard the names they called—
"Buzz" and "Chrome Dome" and "Popeye," too!
What's a kid with long hair to do?
How about this—my hair I'll wrap
And cover with a baseball cap,
Or slather it with lots of grease
And spike it into a masterpiece!
Maybe I can roll it in a bun,
Add a hot dog, and have some fun!
Yes, anything—just leave it alone
For at least six weeks—please, postpone!
Dad, it's not funny! Don't start to laugh!
Please, speak to Mom on my behalf!
What can I do? What do you need—
For me on bended knee to plead?

Ohhh! Today's haircut is not for me!
It's for Mutt, our brand new puppy!
In that case...
Mutt, do not shiver and do not shake.
Getting a haircut is a piece of cake!
Stand up! Be proud! Hold your head up tall.
Don't be a baby and start to bawl!
You'll be a grown-up dog some day,
And a haircut will seem like puppy's play!

1. Circle the main idea of the poem.

   reading a calendar   different hairstyles

   not wanting a haircut

2. Circle all the correct answers.

   You can guess that the speaker probably . . .

   exaggerates.   dislikes haircuts.   wants to become a barber.

   has long hair.   is glad it's the puppy's turn for a haircut.

3. Use the clues to complete the crossword puzzle.

Across

2. an opposite of shrink
4. to use a lot of
8. a great work of art
9. hairless

Down

1. to delay
3. to plead
5. to tremble
6. oily matter
7. to cry loudly

Reptile with a Smile

Line up 7 or 8 yardsticks, and you will see the approximate length of some of the largest crocodiles! This reptile lies low in the water and imitates an old, floating log. Although it may appear to be harmless as it floats along, a crocodile is ready to snap up almost any animal. It is carnivorous—eating fish and frogs whole and dragging larger prey like deer underwater where it bites down and spins rapidly.

While the crocodile and the alligator are often mistaken for each other, there are several characteristics that differ between the two animals. Crocodiles have larger and narrower heads than alligators. Crocodiles are also faster and more graceful both on land and in the water. Another distinguishing feature is their teeth. When a crocodile closes its mouth, the large fourth tooth on each side of the lower jaw is clearly visible. An alligator has no visible lower teeth when its mouth is closed.

An interesting trait of the crocodile is its famous *crocodile smile*. A crocodile remains still in the sun with its mouth open. By doing this the mouth absorbs the sun's heat. This raises the body temperature of the animal, providing it with energy to hunt later at night.

1. Circle the correct animal in each sentence.

   a. When **an alligator / a crocodile** clamps down its jaws, no lower teeth are visible.

   b. **An alligator's / A crocodile's** head is more massive although it is more tapered.

   c. **An alligator / A crocodile** absorbs the sun's heat through its open mouth to convert into energy for later activities.

   d. **An alligator / A crocodile** moves swiftly in water and on land.

2. Complete each statement by circling the correct answer.

   a. Because a crocodile is carnivorous…

      it eats animals like fish and frogs.

      it must drag its food in the water before chewing.

   b. Because a crocodile often imitates an old, floating log…

      it can remain afloat undisturbed for long periods of time.

      it can surprise its unsuspecting prey.

   c. Because a crocodile remains still in the sun with an open mouth…

      it is known for its crocdile smile.

      it catches insects.

Glorious Mud!

Rain, rain, go away!
Jimmy and I want to play.
Jimmy, Jimmy, come and see
A puddle just for you and me!
But...
Mom said, "Don't get your clothes or shoes muddy!"
So I've got a plan—Come here, good buddy.
We'll put our clothes in the box nearby;
Change into our shorts so our clothes stay dry;
Then lay our shoes inside the door.
We won't leave shoe prints on the floor.
So...
We crept outside. It seemed a flood
Had left mounds and mounds of dirty mud.
We wiggled and waggled and splished and splashed.
From puddle to puddle we darted and dashed.
Mudballs flew! Some hit their mark.
Like the one in my face—everything went dark!
We laughed and giggled and jumped and hopped.
Then Jimmy stood frozen. His movement stopped.
Our hearts pounding, we raced in the door.
Gathering our shoes from off the floor.
We washed our feet and our faces.
Mom wouldn't know 'bout our secret places.

Then the door opened—Mom stared at us.
"Boys, there's something that we need to discuss!"
You didn't get muddy—I can clearly see that,
But about the footprints we have to chat!"

Circle each correct answer.

1. In the poem how many children had watched the rain?

       one   two   several

2. Mom's instructions were: "Don't get . . . _____!"

       wet   silly   muddy

3. Everything went dark when . . .

    the speaker was hit by a mudball.

    the lights went out in the storm.

    the speaker dropped his glasses.

4. What are "mounds and mounds?"

      drops   balls   heaps

5. What clue helped Mom realize what her children had done?

  muddy shoe prints   muddy footprints   a pile of dirty clothes

6. Match the two words that have similar meanings by writing the corresponding letter in the blank.

    _____ darted   a. collecting

    _____ discuss   b. talk

    _____ frozen   c. desire

    _____ secret   d. motionless

    _____ want   e. dashed

    _____ gathering   f. hidden

Advice from an Alien

Yesterday was definitely not the best day in Murphy's life. Not only did he fail to do his chores, but he arrived home very late after playing in the park. His parents were upset, and Murphy had to spend the remainder of the day in his room.

"One day everyone is going to be very sorry!" warned Murphy. "I'll just run away from home, and they'll never see me again," he continued as he belly-flopped onto his unmade bed. He proceeded to moan and groan as the night grew darker. Fantasizing where he would rather be at the moment, Murphy stared out the window.

Just then bright lights flashed! Something very strange was happening outside his bedroom window. Murphy carefully climbed out, held onto the ledge, and let himself drop gently to the ground. He walked toward the light.

Almost immediately a small purple creature with long antennae appeared and began to speak.

"My name is Oogo," he began. Then the space creature explained how he had left home after arguing with his parents. That's when he decided to explore the universe.

Murphy replied, "That sounds like great fun. May I join you? I need to get away from my parents. I need my space!"

After a short conversation, Murphy and Oogo decided to climb into Murphy's room so he could gather some things for the trip.

"Wow!" exclaimed Oogo as he carefully studied Murphy's bedroom and all of his belongings. "Your parents must really care

about you. I think I'll go back to my planet and my parents. Murphy, you are one lucky kid!"

"Well, I guess I am," said Murphy as he realized the truth in that statement. He waved good-bye to his new long-distance friend. "There's no place like home!"

_____

1. Write two ways in which Murphy and Oogo were the same and two ways in which they were different.

Same	Different
a. _____	a. _____
_____	_____
b. _____	b. _____
_____	_____

2. Explain what Murphy meant when he said: "There's no place like home."

_____

_____

3. Circle the main idea in the story.

Murphy wanted to run away from home.

Murphy and Oogo were both different, yet similar.

Children should do all of their chores and listen to their parents.

Mammoth Mammals

Amazingly, the largest animal ever recorded is a blue whale! One female blue whale that was caught weighed 190 tons (380,000 pounds)!

Although it is such an enormous creature, a whale is usually very gentle, graceful, and intelligent. It swims by moving its tail up and down, unlike a fish which moves its tail from side to side. Because a whale breathes air, it must swim to the surface of the water. Here it breathes out warm, moist air that mixes with the cool clean air. This creates a whale's famous watery spout. Underwater, a whale can hold its breath for up to an hour.

Whales are warm-blooded and have practically no hair. Instead, they have thick layers of fatty blubber under their smooth skin to keep them warm.

A whale makes a lot of different sounds that can carry many miles through the water. Therefore a young whale cannot ignore its mother when she calls to it to come home!

Whales are now protected so that they do not become extinct. Countries may catch them if they wish to study them for scientific reasons. Sometimes whales get confused as to where they are and get stranded at low tides on beaches. When that happens, people try to keep them alive until the next high tide comes and they can float back out to deeper water. Then they can swim away and resume their journey.

Circle the correct answers.

1. Which traits describe a whale?

    intelligent   clumsy   gentle   slow-witted

    graceful   enormous   warm-blooded   rough skin

2. What is the purpose of blubber?

    It adds to the beauty of the whale.

    It keeps the whale warm.

    It helps a whale use its spout.

Use words from the story and the clues to complete the crossword puzzle.

Across

2. very large water mammals
5. takes in air
6. gigantic
7. non-violent; calm

Down

1. a tool used to measure weight
3. top of the water
4. written down
6. died out

What's in a Name?

Billy and his sister Tammy were always fighting. They would argue about who got the larger dessert. They would yell about who had permission to choose the television program. They would quarrel about who got to be first when they played a game. When they were extremely angry, they would call each other names. Every time they squabbled, their mother became upset. "Children," she would begin, "cross names can be dangerous. You can never be certain what will happen if words are said in anger." The children would quiet down, but this would only last until their next argument.

One day Billy and Tammy's squabbling became so intense that they began calling each other names again.

"Tammy," shouted Billy, "you're dumber than a dodo bird!"

Tammy retorted quickly, "And you're smellier than an ole skunk!"

Then something very strange happened. Tammy turned into a very big and quite ugly dodo bird, and her brother became a very stinky skunk! The two former children stared in amazement.

Just then their mother appeared. "Billy . . . Tammy!" she called, but all she saw were these two very curious-looking creatures. "Where are my children?" she wondered, beginning to worry.

At that moment the children reappeared! They were quite relieved to be themselves. "Mom was right," they agreed. "Name-calling can be dangerous!"

1. Explain this statement: "Sticks and stones may break my bones but names will never hurt me!"

   _____

   _____

   _____

   Do you agree? _____ Why or why not? _____

   _____

   _____

2. Complete this "nice word" puzzle with words from the Word Bank.

Word Bank

admire
appreciate
compliment
encourage
love
share

Top This Toy!

We know that all work and no play can make a person dull, dull, dull! Some people have extraordinary ways to keep from becoming dull.

Many girls like to play with dolls. One female is especially fond of this hobby. Her name is Apryl Scott. Maybe she will let you play with her rag doll. But you probably should bring along a ladder—her doll is almost 42 feet high!

Maybe you like to relax by puttting together jigsaw puzzles. This activity can make time pass quickly. How about trying to fit almost 44,000 pieces together like one made in France?

Another way to relieve boredom is to start collecting gum wrappers to begin making a chain. Perhaps one day you will be able to beat the record gum-wrapper chain—18,721 feet long! It took over 30 years to complete. A record like that makes you wonder who chewed all that gum!

When the weather is cold, children often have fun building snowmen. People in Japan are no different. Some Japanese spent 10 days and nights creating a snowman over $96\frac{1}{2}$ feet tall! This Frosty definitely did not have to hurry on his way for fear of melting away in a short time.

No matter how you play, it should be fun and safe for all. However, don't forget that all play and no work can make a person lazy, lazy, lazy. Find a happy medium and do both with enthusiasm.

Use each clue to fill in the blank with the correct word.

a. _____ owns an enormous rag _____.
        (who)   (what)

   It is almost 42 _____ tall.
                        (what)

b. Jigsaw _____ can be difficult to do,
                  (what)

   especially when the people in _____ create one.
                                      (where)

   Theirs had almost 44,000 _____ .
                              (what)

c. A gum-wrapper _____ can be fun to make. All that
                          (what)

   you need to do is chew lots of _____ , save the
                                (what)

   _____ , and fold them together.
            (what)

d. On a snowy day it can be fun to build a _____ .
                                        (what)

   The more _____ that you use, the bigger it will
                  (what)

   become. Some people in _____ used lots of
                            (where)

   _____ to create a very, very large
        (what)

   _____ .
        (what)

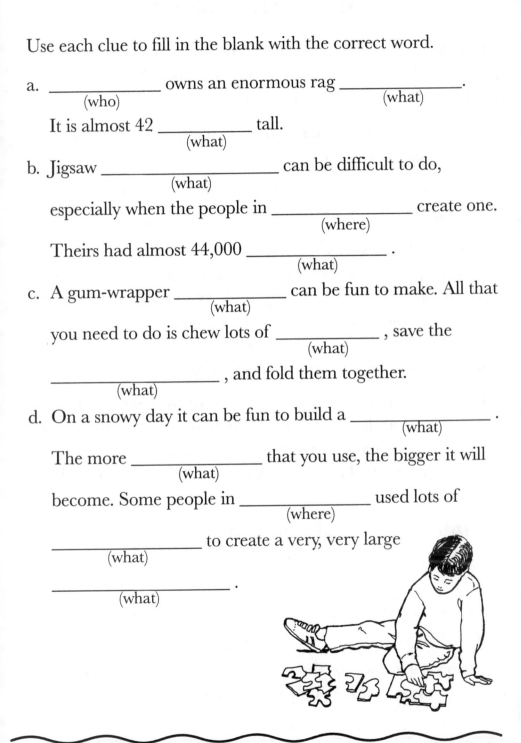

The Clean Machine

Tommy was always spilling food on the floor. He never bothered picking up the crumbs or wiping up the mess unless he was reminded. Of course, this upset his parents.

One day his mother warned him, "Tommy, terrible things can happen when someone is untidy."

"Yes, Tommy," his dad continued, "and you'll have to suffer the consequences of your actions."

Tommy listened politely to their advice. However, he forgot their message when he decided to go downstairs for a late night treat. He tiptoed to the cupboard and began making the gooiest peanut butter and jelly sandwich ever. Gobs of peanut butter and grape jelly fell on the floor. It was soon joined by a huge puddle of spilled milk. Unfazed, Tommy began to eat.

Tommy stopped chewing when he heard what seemed to be tiny footsteps beneath his chair. Tommy bent down and found himself staring at the face of a hideous Monster Mess-Maker! Its long, green tongue slurped noisily across its pointy, yellow teeth. Tommy screamed and raced upstairs.

His parents awoke, and Tommy explained what had happened. When they went into the kitchen, they found the room totally covered with peanut butter, grape jelly, and milk!

"We warned you, son!" they chimed loudly. "If you don't clean up your mess, strange creatures will add to it!"

Tommy spent most of the night cleaning the dirty kitchen. To this day, Tommy immediately wipes up any spills.

Fill in the circle beside the correct answer(s).

1. This story is . . .

   ○ factual.

   ○ fiction.

2. What statement supports your first answer?

   ○ Some boys do make messes.

   ○ Monster Mess-Makers do not exist.

   ○ Parents want their children to be neat.

3. Which details describe the mess in the kitchen?

   ○ gobs of peanut butter and grape jelly

   ○ pointy, yellow teeth

   ○ a huge puddle of spilled milk

   ○ eyes that glow bright orange

   ○ tiny footsteps

4. In which situation(s) would Tommy's Monster Mess-Maker return?

   ○ a neat and tidy chest of drawers

   ○ melting ice cream dripping off the counter

   ○ paint spilling from a can on the basement floor

   ○ a tipped-over bowl of popcorn

   ○ a well-made bed

   ○ clothes thrown on the closet floor

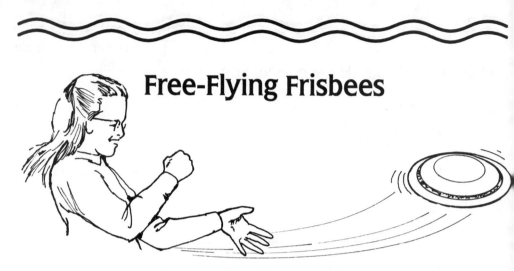

Free-Flying Frisbees

The next time you toss a Frisbee, you may envision it containing a pie or little men from outer space. That little disk has an interesting history.

In the 1870s a man named William Russell Frisbie opened a bakery in Connecticut. For his homemade pies, Mr. Frisbie used tin pie pans that were embossed with his family name. As the years progressed, students from nearby Yale University began flinging these pie pans in lawn games.

Then in the 1950s Walter Frederick Morrison developed a toy which he hoped would intrigue flying saucer/UFO enthusiasts like himself. It was first constructed as a metal toy disk but later was changed to plastic. Mr. Morrison joined Wham-O Company and sold these toys as "Flyin' Saucers." In 1959, the president of Wham-O changed the name of the toy to *Frisbee* (with the spelling changed) after he discovered students at Yale and Harvard tossing Frisbie metal pie pans around as their predecessors had done in the mid-1940s.